MW01203960

Alabama Tailgate Cookbook, 2010 Recipes in Review

Published by Shane Hill
tsquareevents@gmail.com
Birmingham, AL
www.alabamatailgate.com

ISBN - 978-1461104520

Cover Design - LeeAnn Ramey, Ramey Design, Birmingham, AL, rameydesign@charter.net

Cover Photos – Shane and Julie Hill, Birmingham, AL

First Printing May 2011

Dedication

First and foremost, to Mom: You taught me well, and I think about you every time I am in the kitchen.

Julie, my wife and best friend: You put up with me packing the truck out like the Beverly Hillbillies and trekking to Tuscaloosa for all the home games. I love you and thank you for your support.

Acknowledgements

Dad, thanks for spending your weekends with us in Tuscaloosa and being so supportive of my hobby.

The whole Jarmon crew – thank you, I am very grateful for the hospitality and outdoor kitchen.

Tailgate friends and supporters – ya'll keep coming back, so I must be doing something right.

Contents

Introduction

Can I have the recipe? Where did you get this idea from? How do you feed this many people? How long did this take you? Why do you do this?

The questions posed above are what I hear most often on Saturdays in the fall for each of the Alabama home football games. So, I thought I would answer a few of these as well as give you my recipes for the entire 2010 Alabama Football season.

I love to cook, I love the process. From planning to shopping, from setup to prep and from prep to cooking, I love it all (well, I may not be crazy about the cleaning up). There is something very gratifying about taking a pile of raw ingredients and turning it into a finished product and actually watching people enjoy your creation.

I grew up with a stay at home mom who was a great cook. I was always in the kitchen with her when I was young watching and learning. Fast forward to 1992 and I found myself living in an apartment for college. I quickly grew tired of hamburger helper and started trying to learn how to cook. My mother sent me off with a box of recipes and the following advice: "You can cook just about anything you want one of two ways, boil it in water for 30 minutes or cook it at 350 degrees in the oven for 30 minutes". She cautioned that it would not be very good, but it would be cooked. So, I started cooking some of the recipes she sent me, as well as reading cookbooks. From 1992 – 2000 I spent more and more time in the kitchen. I learned what ingredients worked well together and what did not. From there I have continued to grow and learn every time I cook or read a cooking magazine or cookbook.

Those of you who have been to my tailgates know that I try to keep things interesting with fresh tailgate themes and ideas. For 2010 I decided to try and work a local Alabama product into each of the home games to help highlight and support our Alabama farmers and businesses.

So how does all that get us to the cookbook? In 2009 I started earning my masters degree from UAB in the Information Engineering Management program. We spent a fair deal of time working on finding a passion and developing it into a product. This is my product. I hope that you enjoy the quick stories about the tailgates and find the recipes delicious and fun to cook.

Thanks for your support and Roll Tide.

Shane Hill

What This Book Is and What It Is Not

For my tailgates, it is not uncommon to cook for 100 people. As a result, my recipes get scaled up and down as needed.

This book is not an exact science, a recipe to follow and never modify. You will notice that quite often I will specify salt and pepper or some other spice "to taste". Well, that is exactly what I mean. Think another ingredient would be better, give it a try. If you like it, email it to me and I will give it a try. It may make the next book! Chances are I tweaked the recipe in some way based on my mood, the weather or what I had on hand at the tailgate.

I have read and re-read every recipe multiple times, but try as much as I may I am sure a few things slipped past me and the editor.

These recipes are my starting points and will be just fine as they are documented, but do not be afraid to experiment.

Feel free to give me feedback on the book's website (www.alabamatailgate.com).

Game 1 - Alabama vs. San Jose State

Early season games are always so hard to cook for. In Alabama it is still in the mid 90's for the first few games. I wanted something that would beat the heat, yet still be filling enough for a main meal.

For the local Alabama ingredient I choose watermelon. I liked the idea of the refreshing nature of watermelon and came up with some interesting menu items in order to keep it fresh and new.

I wanted also to play into the California angle for San Jose State. I decided on sushi and came up with two recipes. The first was a take on the California Roll, but instead of trying to make that for 75 people, I chose to do a salad. The next was a Ceviche, but I did not want raw fish out in the heat so I found a cooked recipe.

Pair the sushi items with some watermelon and here is what I came up with.

Lunch

- Watermelon Margaritas
- California Roll Tide Roll Salad
- Watermelon, Feta and Basil Salad
- Pork Tenderloin with a Watermelon BBQ Sauce.
- Cooked Shrimp Ceviche Cocktail

Watermelon Margaritas

These drinks offer a twist on an old standby. Be sure to taste as you go and read through the directions before you start. I mix this up in a large drink cooler and add ice to keep it cold for everyone.

2 large seedless watermelons

2 gallons water (split into gallons)

10 cups sugar

10 limes (more if desired)

Shane Hill

1.5 liters white tequila

1.5 liters gold tequila

750 ml Triple Sec

1. Cut melons into chunks and puree in a blender or food processor. Place puree in the refrigerator.
2. Zest and juice all 10 limes.
3. Combine one gallon of water, sugar and lime zest in a stock pot. Bring to a boil while stirring. Cook until sugar dissolves. Allow to cool to room temp and strain zest. Add sugar lime water to large serving container.
4. Add watermelon puree and lime juice from 10 limes to container with sugar lime water.
5. Add remaining gallon of water and taste. The mixture should be slightly sweet from the watermelon and tangy from the lime.
6. Add tequila and 1/2 the bottle of Triple Sec and stir.
7. Taste and adjust with more lime juice or Triple Sec. Add lime to get more zing and Triple Sec to get more sweetness.
8. Serve over ice and enjoy!

California 'Roll Tide Roll' Salad

This salad was a huge hit. It is nice and refreshing with a great texture. Be sure to keep it chilled right up until you serve it.

2 cups uncooked white rice

4 cups of beer or water

1 inch section of ginger root, grated

2 small heads iceberg lettuce, sliced

3 English cucumbers, diced into 1/2" cubes

4 avocados, pitted and diced into 1/2" cubes

8 cups imitation crabmeat, diced into 1/2" cubes

8 teaspoons wasabi powder, or to taste

1/4 cup mayonnaise

1/4 cup soy sauce

1/2 cup rice wine vinegar

1/4 cup white sugar

4 teaspoons sesame oil

1. Bring 4 cups water or beer to boil and add rice. Cover and reduce heat to simmer. Cook 20 minutes. Remove from heat and let cool.
2. Combine cooled rice, ginger, lettuce, avocados, crab meat and cucumbers
3. In a small bowl mix mayonnaise, soy, vinegar, sugar, wasabi powder and oil
4. Toss salad with sauce

Watermelon, Feta and Basil Salad

The feta really adds a nice salty zing to the watermelon. I toss it in the balsamic vinegar right before I serve. Make sure to use fresh basil in this one.

1 large seedless watermelon

2 pounds feta, crumbled

10 fresh basil leaves

Couple of dashes of balsamic vinegar

1. Remove watermelon from rind and slice into 1" cubes
2. Dice Basil leaves
3. Combine Watermelon, feta and basil and gently mix
4. Sprinkle with balsamic vinegar
5. Chill for one hour

Grilled Spiced Pork Tenderloin with Watermelon BBQ Sauce

The pork alone is great, no sauce needed. It is super simple and economical for a large group. It has some kick to it, but not enough to scare everyone off.

For the pork:

Shane Hill

2 pork tenderloins

4 tablespoons Montreal Steak Seasoning

1 tablespoon Cajun seasoning

2 teaspoons olive oil

1. Place pork tenderloins in a Ziploc bag and add olive oil. Toss to coat. Add Montreal Steak Seasoning and Cajun spice, massage into pork.
2. Heat grill with a hot fire on one side and low fire on the other. Sear on all 4 sides over hot fire. Move to low fire and grill for 15-20 minutes. Internal temp should be 145 degrees when you pull it from the fire.
3. Allow to rest under a foil tent for 5 minutes. Slice and serve with Watermelon BBQ Sauce.

For Watermelon BBQ Sauce

This sauce really is more a traditional BBQ sauce with a hint of watermelon. Give it a try on pork or chicken.

Rind from 1/2 small watermelon

1 cup corn syrup

1/2 cup water

1/4 cup Ketchup

1/4 cup apple cider vinegar

1 teaspoon crushed red pepper flakes

1/2 teaspoon liquid smoke

1 teaspoon black pepper

1. Cut away green section and 1/2 inch of white from rind. Leaving the pink and some white of the rind. Add pink and white rind to food processor and puree, discard the green section.
2. Strain liquid from pulp and reserve pulp (discard liquid). You should have about 1/2 to 3/4 of a cup of pulp.
3. Combine pulp and all other ingredients in a sauce pan.

4. Bring to a boil and then reduce heat to a simmer. Place lid on sauce pan and simmer for 45 minutes, stirring from time to time. Remove lid and simmer until thick.

Cooked Shrimp Ceviche Cocktail

People loved this dish. The ingredients combine to add a nice kick. It can be served warm or cold, but chilled on a hot day is really nice.

1 quart salted water

1/2 cup plus 2 tablespoons freshly squeezed lime juice

1 pound unpeeled medium shrimp

1/2 medium white onion, chopped into 1/4-inch pieces

1/3 cup chopped fresh cilantro, plus several sprigs for garnish

1/2 cup ketchup

1 to 2 tablespoons vinegary Mexican hot sauce

About 2 tablespoons olive oil

1 cup diced cucumber

1 small ripe avocado, peeled, pitted and cubed

Salt, to taste

1. Bring 1 quart salted water to a boil and add 2 tablespoons of the lime juice. Add shrimp, cover and return to a boil. Immediately remove from heat, drain
2. Add shrimp to large glass serving dish
3. Add remaining ingredients and toss to coat
4. Chill and serve

Game 2 - Alabama vs. Penn State

I was still looking for menu items that helped beat the heat, but also worked into the Penn State theme. The temperature for this game dropped a few degrees, but was still hot working the grill. I also knew that we were going to have a huge crowed for this one and I wanted to be sure to have plenty of food. We had a late kick off so we decided to do a brunch and late lunch.

For the local ingredient, I featured cheese from Wright Dairy located right here in Alabama. To bring a little Penn State into the menu, I went with a variation of a cheese steak and paid homage to the Dutch influence of Pennsylvania serving up some sausages on pretzel rolls.

Brunch

- Roll Tide Crimson Mimosas
- Assorted meats, cheeses, fruits and veggies – no recipe here, just buy them and set out a tray
- Pita chips with roasted red pepper feta dip

Lunch

- Bayou Ribeye Rolls with Cheese
- Various Grilled German / Dutch Sausage on Pretzel Rolls
- Grilled German Potato Salad with a Bacon Vinaigrette
- Tomato, Mozzarella, Salami and Basil Salad
- Chilled Cucumber Salsa

Roll Tide Crimson Mimosas

Here is a twist on an old brunch favorite.

750 ml chilled champagne

750 ml chilled cranberry juice

1. Combine and serve.

Roasted Red Pepper and Feta Dip

This dish is always a hit. Roasting the peppers gives the dish a nice twist and depth. It is also great as a grilled cheese. The taste and texture is somewhere between hummus and pimento cheese.

4 red peppers

1 pound feta cheese, crumbled

1 cup olive oil

Juice of 1 lemon

Salt and pepper to taste

1. Roast red peppers, place on hot grill and char on all sides. Remove from heat and place in Ziploc bag and let cool
2. Once cool remove skin and seeds and tear into quarters
3. Place peppers in food processor and purée
4. Add feta to processor and pulse 2 seconds 4 times
5. Turn processor on and drizzle in olive oil until it has the consistency of hummus
6. Add lemon juice to taste
7. Salt and Pepper to taste

Bayou Ribeye Rolls

These offer a nice take on the traditional Philly Cheese steak. The Cajun spice gives them a nice kick. I am not a fan of peppers on my Philly's and do not use them here. The Penn State fans loved them. Be sure to use good quality steak for these.

3 pounds ribeye steak thin sliced (ask your butcher to slice the meat for Philly Cheese Steaks)

12 hoagie rolls

12 slices provolone cheese

Shane Hill

3 onions julienned

3 tablespoons Cajun seasoning

4 tablespoons olive oil

1. Rub 1 tablespoon oil on steak
2. Rub Cajun seasoning over steak
3. Heat large cast iron skillet over medium - high heat
4. Add 2 tablespoons oil to the skillet and brown steaks in skillet, cook until medium and remove from heat
5. Once all steaks are cooked, add 1 tablespoon oil back to skillet and caramelize onions. Scrape the pan as the juices from the onion loosens the bits of steak. If there is not enough juice in the onion, add about 1/4 cup beer
6. While onions are cooking dice the cooked steak and place on a roll with cheese
7. When the onions are done, top the cheese with onions

Various Grilled German / Dutch Sausages on Pretzel Rolls

The pretzel rolls give a nice flavor to these and are super easy to make and eat. Be sure to pick good quality mustard.

3 pounds of various sausages – if you are here in Birmingham, hit Klingler's in Vestavia.

24 pretzel rolls

Good Quality Spicy Mustard

1. Poach sausages in pan of water for about 20 minutes. This cooks them without drying them out.
2. Finish on the grill for about 5 minutes getting a good sear on all sides.
3. Slice and serve on pretzel rolls with mustard.

Tailgate German Potato Salad with Bacon Vinaigrette

I think this was the most requested recipe from the Penn State game. The shrimp boil gives the potatoes a nice flavor. If you have time, slice the potatoes after boiling them for 7 minutes and finish them on the grill.

4 pounds of red potatoes

4 tablespoons powdered shrimp boil

1 pound apple smoked bacon, cut into 1" pieces

2 small onions, diced

4 cloves garlic, diced

4 tablespoons Dijon mustard

1/4 cup olive oil

1/4 cup balsamic vinegar

Salt / pepper to taste

1. Fill stock pot with enough water to cover potatoes by 3", add shrimp boil and bring to a boil
2. Add potatoes, return to a boil and cook for 20 minutes (drain when done)
3. While potatoes are cooking, brown bacon in a dutch oven
4. Kill heat, remove bacon and drain off grease into a bowl (keeping grease) – leave 1 tablespoon in the dutch oven
5. Once removed grease has cooled - whisk in oil and vinegar
6. Bring Dutch oven back up to medium - high. Brown onions and add garlic, cook for one more minute
7. Add potatoes to onion mixture and roughly mash them with a wooden spoon
8. Add vinaigrette, bacon pieces and Dijon mustard – stir
9. Salt and Pepper to taste

Tomato, Mozzarella, Salami, and Basil Salad

This is a quick dish that can be made the night before and tossed right before serving.

4 heirloom tomatoes, seeded, cored and diced

1 pound Salami, cut into 1/4" dice

4 fresh basil leaves, diced

1 pound whole smoked mozzarella, 1/4" diced (regular mozzarella is alright if you cannot get smoked)

2 tablespoons olive oil

Shane Hill

2 tablespoons balsamic vinegar

1. Combine all ingredients and toss

Chilled Cucumber Salsa

I was not sure about this dish at first, but it turned out great. I liked the idea of using chilled cucumbers since they are so refreshing. The dill adds a nice flavor to the dish.

2 medium cucumbers - peeled, seeded, and chopped

2 medium tomatoes - seeded, cored and chopped

1/2 cup diced green bell pepper

1 jalapeño pepper - seeded and minced

1 small onion - diced

1 clove garlic - minced

2 tablespoons lime juice

1 teaspoon minced fresh parsley

2 teaspoons minced fresh cilantro

1/2 teaspoon dried dill weed

1/2 teaspoon salt

1. Combine and toss

Game 3 - Alabama vs. Duke

Game three welcomed our first road game of the year. I ended up out of town that weekend without a kitchen. Since I was not at home to cook for this one I thought I would throw out some favorite tailgate items from years gone by and a drink recommendation.

The redneck sushi is always a hit and one of the most requested recipes. Oysters are quite easy to prepare, and since they open when cooked you do not need to worry about having someone dedicated to shucking them.

Lunch

- Blue Devil Cocktails
- Redneck Sushi
- Fire Roasted Oysters
- Spicy Cocktail Sauce

Blue Devil Cocktails

Careful with this drink, it is pretty strong.

1/2 ounce rum

1/2 ounce gin

1/2 ounce gold tequila

1/2 ounce vodka

1/2 ounce Grand Marnier

1/2 ounce Blue Curacao

3 ounces pineapple juice

1. Fill shaker half full of ice
2. Add all ingredients to shaker
3. Shake well

4. Strain and serve

Redneck Sushi

I first had a variation of this dish at a beer festival from a high end restaurant. They used a traditional southern slaw. I added the ginger dressing, hot sauce and mustard. My friend Charlie Stevens recommended the sesame seeds and they add a nice touch. Don't let the fact that they are based on a corn dog scare you, people love this dish.

10 corn dogs, fried or baked (you need the crunch)

1 package of angel hair slaw

2 bottles of soy ginger dressing

3 tablespoons sesame seeds

Sriracha hot sauce

Wasabi mustard

1. Once corndogs are cooked, remove stick and slice into 1/2" pieces
2. Mix slaw and dressing
3. Place 1 tablespoon of slaw on top of each slice of corndog
4. Dot each slice with hot sauce and mustard
5. Sprinkle with sesame seeds
6. Serve and enjoy

Fire Roasted Oysters

Make sure to get burlap that is not colored with dye or any print on it. You can pick this up at a fabric store. Soak it very well in water.

2 dozen oysters in the shell

6 foot x 2 foot section of burlap sack, soaked in water

1. Heat a grill to medium – high
2. Wash oysters
3. Place oysters on grill
4. Cover grill / oysters with burlap

5. Check oysters every 5 minutes
6. When they open, they are done
7. Remove and enjoy (The shells are hot!)

Spicy Cocktail Sauce

Adjust this with more or less horseradish as needed. People have told me my recipe is the best sinus clearing medicine known.

32 ounces ketchup

16 ounces horseradish (more if you like it even hotter)

4 tablespoons worcestershire sauce

4 tablespoons hot sauce

2 lemons, juiced

1. Combine all ingredients in a bowl and mix
2. Add more horseradish if you want more heat
3. Serve with oysters

Game 4 - Alabama vs. Arkansas

Game four brought us our second away game. This marked the first away game of 2010 where I was going to be at home in my kitchen. Since this was an afternoon game, we decided to have folks over and provide a late lunch. Playing the Hogs always calls for some kind of pork. Last year I cooked a whole hog at the tailgate, but decided to scale it back this time.

I have traditionally always cooked BBQ in a smoker. However, since my wife bought me a new Weber Summit 670, I decided to give the smoke box and rotisserie a try for this menu.

Of this menu, I think the beans were the hands-down favorite.

Lunch

- Rotisserie Pork Butt
- Dry Rubbed Ribs
- Strawberry BBQ Sauce
- Razorback Beans

Rotisserie Pork Butt

This was the first time I tried the pork butt on the rotisserie. I kept the rotisserie burner on long enough to get a nice sear on the pork. I then kicked on the side burners away from the meat to hold the grill at 215 degrees while keeping the smoke box filled with wet wood chips. You can always sear and then smoke the butt for about 30 minutes and finish it off in an oven.

1 pork butt

1 recipe BBQ rub (recipe follows)

4 ounces apple juice

4 ounces vinegar

4 ounces beer

4 tablespoons olive oil

1. Remove pork from refrigerator and let sit at room temperature for 20 minutes.
2. Coat pork butt with olive oil
3. Coat outside of pork butt with BBQ rub
4. Skewer pork with rotisserie
5. Place rotisserie on grill with aluminum pan under pork, fill pan with liquids
6. Place wood chips in smoke box (or foil packet if your grill does not have a smoke box)
7. Kick grill on medium, with rotisserie burner on high. Cook until a nice crust forms from rotisserie burner
8. Kill rotisserie burner and use indirect burners to hold grill temp at 210 – 225 degrees
9. Cook for one and a half hours per pound, or until meat reaches 195 degrees
10. Remove from heat and allow to cool
11. Shred when ready to serve

BBQ Rub

This is my base recipe. I taste and adjust as I go. Add more heat or more sugar depending on what taste you are after. This makes a large batch, but will keep well. Pull out what you think you will need for a batch and make sure not to cross contaminate back to the storage container.

1 cup dark brown sugar

1/2 cup garlic powder

1/2 cup kosher salt

1/2 cup hot paprika

2 tablespoons onion powder

1 tablespoon hot mustard powder

1 tablespoon Cajun seasoning

1 tablespoon chili powder

1 tablespoon red pepper

Shane Hill

1 tablespoon cumin

1 tablespoon black pepper

1. Mix everything making sure to break up the lumps of brown sugar
2. Store in an airtight container

Dry Rubbed Ribs

Some people love dry ribs, some hate them. If you would rather have them wet, then finish them with sauce.

2 racks baby back ribs

BBQ dry rub

2 tablespoons olive oil

Squirt bottle filled with 50/50 mixture of apple cider vinegar and apple juice

3 tablespoons olive oil

1. Remove thin membrane from back of ribs
2. Coat ribs with olive oil and then rub on dry rub
3. Heat grill to medium - high. Sear ribs on each side
4. Place wood chips in smoke box (or foil packet if your grill does not have a smoke box)
5. Reduce heat to 225 – 250 degrees, cook ribs via indirect heat turning every 30 minutes. At each turn, spray with apple juice and vinegar
6. Grill for 2 hours keeping smoke going the whole time
7. After 2 hours, wrap ribs in foil (spray them one last time) and cook for 4 more hours at 225 – 250 degrees

Razorback Beans

This is another dish that always seems to rank high on the request list. Some people like to use BBQ or hamburger for the meat, but I found that breakfast sausage works really well. For the beans I like to use Bush's in the green can.

1 pound hot breakfast sausage

1 tablespoon olive oil

1 red bell pepper, chopped

1 onion, chopped

2 cloves garlic, chopped

2 (28-ounce) cans baked beans

1/4 cup brown sugar

1/4 cup molasses

1 cup BBQ sauce

1. Add oil to hot dutch oven
2. Sauté onions and garlic
3. Add sausage and brown
4. Drain grease
5. Add beans and all other ingredients
6. Place lid on dutch oven and reduce heat to simmer.
7. Simmer for 1 hour.

Strawberry BBQ Sauce

I came up with this recipe a few years back when my friend Denny (who is an excellent cook) decided we should do an Iron Chef Style tailgate. We both walked away from that tailgate with several dishes that made the normal rotation. Strawberries were one of the ingredients and here is what I came up with.

1 small onion, diced

1 clove garlic, minced

4 cups ketchup

1/4 cup vinegar

1/2 cup olive oil

8 ounces strawberry jam

Shane Hill

1/4 cup honey

1/2 can beer

2 tablespoons worcestershire sauce

2 tablespoons black pepper

1 tablespoon garlic salt

1 tablespoon onion salt

1 tablespoon cayenne

1. Sauté onion and garlic in 1 teaspoon of the olive oil
2. Add all other remaining ingredients and bring to a boil, reduce heat and simmer for 30 minutes stirring occasionally. Make sure not to scorch.

Game 5 - Alabama vs. Florida

Game five welcomed us back to Tuscaloosa and back to cooking at the tailgate along with the Florida Gators. The week of the game I received some questions on my blog from a fellow Florida blogger about Tuscaloosa tailgating so we arranged to meet up with Hannah and Pete at the tailgate house.

I decided to give a tip of the hat to Florida's Cuban heritage as well as work some of the more traditional Florida items into the menu. In keeping with a local Alabama theme for this tailgate, I included grits from McEwen & Sons as part of the Shrimp / Crawfish and Grits.

Combine all those and a large tailgate and here is the menu.

Brunch and Lunch

- Swamp Juice
- Caramelized Corn Grits Topped with Shrimp and Crawfish
- Hot Sauce Marinated Onion Straws
- Fried Gator Bites (seasoned gator meat lightly fried)
- Cuban Sandwiches
- Ropa Vieja
- Cumin Scented Rice

Swamp Juice

It does not take much OJ to turn these green and thus they are pretty strong. Try adding pineapple or other juices to this cocktail.

2 ounces vodka

4 ounces Blue Curacao

Orange Juice (mix for color)

1. Mix vodka and Blue Curacao over ice
2. Add orange juice while stirring until drink turns green

Shane Hill

Caramelized Corn Grits

A few years back I found McEwen & Sons stone ground grits and have been using them ever since. Adding the fresh corn gives this dish great depth. If you have never made true grits you are missing out. I will caution that when you get all the liquid in the dish you are going to think it is way too thin; it will turn out just fine. I sometimes use a mixture of stock and heavy cream for the cooking liquid.

6 fresh ears of corn, corn removed from cob

2 sweet onions, diced

4 cloves of garlic, minced

1 pound hickory smoked bacon, diced

8 cups chicken stock

2 cups McEwen & Sons Stone Ground Grits

4 tablespoons butter

Salt and pepper to taste

1. In a large dutch oven cook bacon over medium heat until crisp, remove from pan and reserve grease in pan
2. Add onion and corn and cook over medium heat until caramelized, add garlic and cook 1 more minute
3. Salt and pepper to taste
4. Add chicken stock and butter. Bring to a boil, add grits and return to a boil
5. Reduce heat to simmer, cover and cook 25 minutes
6. Stir in cooked bacon
7. Serve with shrimp and crawfish

Shrimp and Crawfish for Grits

This dish has always been a hit and I have been cooking a variation of it for years now. I like to make my own Tasso, but you can order it online or find it in small specialty shops.

1 lb Tasso, diced

1 1/2 pounds andouille sausage, diced

1/4 stick butter

2 onions, diced

4 sticks celery, chopped

1 red pepper, diced

1 cup diced tomato

White wine, to cover

2 lb shrimp, peeled

1/2 pound crawfish tail meat (get it in the frozen seafood section)

3 tablespoons heavy cream

Salt, pepper, Cajun spice, bay leaf

1. In a large Dutch oven cook Tasso and sausage over medium heat for 8 minutes, remove from pan
2. Add butter to pan and sauté veggies, about 8 minutes
3. Add salt, pepper and Cajun spice to taste
4. Add the Tasso and sausage back to the pot
5. Cover with white wine and add bay leaf. Bring to a boil, reduce heat and simmer for 10 minutes
6. Sprinkle shrimp and crawfish with Cajun seasoning
7. Crank the heat back up and bring to a boil, add shrimp and crawfish and return to a boil
8. Reduce heat to simmer and cook until shrimp are done (when they turn pink)
9. Add cream and stir to combine

Hot Sauce Marinated Onion Straws

These are delicious on the top of the shrimp and grits or as a simple side to about anything. They are not as hot as you would think.

2 large sweet onions, julienned

3/4 cup Frank's Hot Sauce

1/4 cup corn meal

Shane Hill

3/4 cup all purpose flour

2 cups peanut oil

Salt, pepper and Cajun seasoning to taste

1. Add onions and hot sauce to zip lock bag and place in refrigerator for 2 hours
2. Remove onions from hot sauce and place in another bag with corn meal, flour and seasoning. Toss to coat
3. Heat oil to 350 degrees in a fryer
4. Remove onions from mixture and shake excess flour mixture off. Add to deep fryer and fry until golden brown

Fried Gator Bites

You can order alligator meat from a number of specialty shops online. For this game, I cooked gator a number of ways. One of them was a package of pre-breaded alligator meat. It turned out great and saved the hassle of prepping at the tailgate. I also cooked a couple of batches of alligator filets on the grill.

1 package of pre-breaded alligator meat

2 cups peanut oil

1. Heat oil to 350 degrees
2. Fry until the nuggets are brown and floating

Cuban Sandwiches

I was introduced to a Cuban sandwich when I lived in Tuscaloosa. The local Winn-Dixie had them in the deli one day, and I gave one a try. From that point forward, I was hooked. As the years went on I have tried them from more authentic sources and to this day it is still one of my favorite foods.

Take the time to find the roast pork; it is one of the keys to this dish.

(3) 1 foot-long crusty Cuban bread loafs

2 tablespoons butter, melted

2 tablespoons olive oil

3 lbs roasted pork, thin sliced

3 lbs smoked ham, thin sliced

1 lb sliced Swiss cheese

30 dill pickle slices

6 tablespoons mayonnaise

6 tablespoons mustard (optional)

1. Slice loafs open and brush inside with the melted butter and olive oil, grill bread buttered side down until lightly brown (very light brown)
2. Slather the bread with the mayonnaise (add the mustard here if you are using it, I do not)
3. Pile equal parts of meat, cheese and pickles on the bread
4. Place sandwich back on the griddle and put a heavy dutch oven on the loaf to press it down. Grill for 1 minute, flip and leave on grill one more minute.
5. Remove, slice into 3" pieces and enjoy

Ropa Vieja

A few years back I decided to cook in the 'Great Customer Cook-off' at The Vintage Wine Shoppe here in Birmingham. For the cook off, you choose a country and cook a dish from that country. The shop paired a wine with your choice. I picked Cuba and decided to cook Ropa Vieja, but decided to use pork since the dish would hold better and stay juicy longer. We won first place with this dish.

Since I had decided to play into the Cuban heritage for the Florida game, this dish seemed to make sense. It holds well, so you can drop the heat down to a simmer and people can grab a bowl whenever they like.

It is also a rather hearty dish and heavy enough for cold games, but fresh enough you can enjoy year round.

A key to this dish is to roast the peppers. It removes some of the heat and gives it an incredible depth at the same time.

By the way, the pork that I cook for this is super easy and a great dish by itself.

5 pounds pork butt

Shane Hill

1/3 cup Hawaiian salt

2 teaspoons liquid smoke

3 cups water

2 1/2 cups veal broth

1 red bell pepper, diced

1 yellow bell pepper, roasted and diced

3 small poblano peppers, 1 roasted and diced – 2 diced

2 Anaheim chile pepper, roasted and diced

4 cubanelle peppers, 2 roasted and diced – 2 diced

2 medium onions, diced

(1) 28 ounce can fire roasted diced tomatoes

4 cloves of garlic, minced

2 tablespoons dried oregano

1 tablespoon ground cumin

2 tablespoons olive oil

Salt and black pepper to taste

1. For the pork, add water and liquid smoke to a roasting pan. Place the pork butt fat side up in the water. Sprinkle with salt. Cover the roasting dish with aluminum foil and roast at 400 degrees for 3 1/2 hours or until done. Reserve cooking liquid
2. Once pork is done, remove from heat and allow to cool. When cooled, remove fat and shred
3. While the above cooks, sauté all non roasted peppers and onions in a large Dutch oven until golden. Add garlic and cook 1 minute more.   Season with salt and pepper to taste
4. Add veal broth and 1/2 cup of the cooking liquid from the pork to the veggie mixture

5. Add oregano, cumin and roasted peppers. Increase heat to high and bring to a boil, reduce heat to a simmer and add shredded pork. Cook 10 minutes

Cumin Scented Rice

This is a quick and easy recipe to give rice a little more flavor. It pairs well with just about any South American meal.

By using stock and beer, I find the rice does not need salt or butter. I like a heavy beer like traditional Budweiser for this dish.

2 cups long grain rice

1 tablespoon olive oil

2 tablespoons whole cumin seed

2 cups chicken stock

2 cups Budweiser beer

1. Heat olive oil over medium-high heat
2. Add cumin seeds and toast, but do not burn (2-3 minutes)
3. Add rice and cook for 1 more minute, stirring the whole time
4. Add liquid and bring to a boil, stir
5. Reduce heat to simmer and cover with tight lid, let cook 22 minutes. Don't peek or check the rice until 22 minutes

Game 6 - Alabama vs. South Carolina

Game six found another weekend that I was not going to be at home or even near a kitchen for that matter. For this reason, I thought I would give you a couple of recipes from the past.

A friend of ours is actually a Clemson graduate, but his wife is a Gamecock alumni. He had us over a few years ago and introduced us to a South Carolinian dish known as Chicken Bog. Chicken Bog is their Jambalaya – no real recipe and as many ways to cook it as there are to pronounce it.

In addition to the Chicken Bog, I thought I would pass along another chicken dish. A few years ago I wanted chicken wings, but not the mess. So, I developed a chicken wing dip. A key here is to use rotisserie chicken and not something out of a can.

All Day Menu

Chicken Bog

No real spice amounts were ever given to me. Here is a base of what I use, but will tone it up or down depending on how hot people want it. This recipe is on the milder side for this dish. With the rice, do not check it as you go. Cover and let the magic happen.

(2) 3 pound bags of long grain white rice

1 box Uncle Ben's Original Wild Rice

1 rotisserie chicken, meat removed

2 pounds smoked sausage, cut into 1/4" rounds (I mix smoked and spicy)

Chicken broth, enough to cook rice (2 1/2 cups of stock to 1 cup of rice)

1 bag of Zatarains brand shrimp boil

4 tablespoons Cajun spice

2 tablespoons garlic powder

2 tablespoons fresh ground black pepper (a key to the dish according to our friend)

3 bay leaves

1. Mix rice and all spices, including spice packet from Uncle Ben's (leave the shrimp boil in the bag) into a large mixing bowl. Mark spot on bowl, you will need 2 1/2 times this amount of stock
2. Measure 2 1/2 times the amount of rice mixture in stock and add to a large cast iron Dutch oven and bring to a boil
3. Remove shrimp boil spice bag
4. Add rice, chicken meat and sausage to stock and stir well and bring to a boil
5. Reduce heat to simmer and put on a tight lid
6. Let cook 22 minutes. Remove lid, stir and enjoy

Buffalo Chicken Wing Dip

This is a quick dip that is super easy to make ahead of time. Everyone loves this dish and I always get at least one request for the recipe. I like to use the blue cheese dressings from the refrigerated isle.

1 Rotisserie chicken, meat removed

16 ounces cream cheese, room temp

(1) 12 oz jar blue cheese dressing

16 ounces hot wing sauce

8 ounces extra sharp cheddar cheese

2 tablespoons of crumbled blue cheese

1. In a bowl mix dressing, cream cheese and wing sauce, stir to combine
2. Add chicken and stir
3. Place mixture in a baking dish and cover with cheddar cheese
4. Sprinkle blue cheese on top
5. Bake at 350 degrees for 20 minutes, or until cheese is bubbly on top
6. Serve with crackers, chips, celery and carrots

Game 7 - Alabama vs. Ole Miss

Ole Miss was homecoming this year, but had an 8 p.m. kickoff. So, people would be coming to campus for the homecoming activities during the day and then have a long wait until the game.

Since I was not sure how many people would drop in at what time, it was hard to plan a meal. Additionally, I was not going to be able to make the tailgate because of school (after all school was the whole inspiration for this book anyway, so I thought I may want to attend class).

I did not want my wife and friends to have to try and cook, so I decided to try a new technique for the game. One where all you had to do was boil water and drop in a bag of food. Twenty minutes later, you have dinner ready. Better yet, you can just open a packet as you are ready to serve and let the rest simmer in the hot water until everyone has finished the last packet.

For this technique, dishes that hold well are ideal since it technically is cooking the dish again. Stews and hearty foods do well with this technique. Given that we were well into the cooler evenings, chili sounded like the perfect dish. Earlier in the week I cooked up about 4 gallons of chili and vacuum sealed it into 1 gallon batches.

A few years back I thought I had the perfect chili recipe. One day I decided to try Dragon's Breath Chili from Guy Fieri on Food Network. I have tweaked this recipe to add a few things and take a few away. It turns out just about perfect every time.

Late Evening No Cook Menu

Shane's Variation of Dragons Breath Chili

Roasting the peppers for this dish is a must. It adds depth and lots of flavor. Be sure to use fresh quality spices as well. The ingredients list is long, but much of that is spice and needed. Do not let that scare you off, this is a great recipe.

4 tablespoons olive oil

2 red bell peppers, diced

2 jalapenos, minced

3 anaheim chilies, roasted, peeled, chopped

3 poblano chilies, roasted, peeled, chopped

2 yellow onions, diced

4 cloves head garlic, minced

1 pound ground veal

2 pounds ground buffalo meat

1 pound hot breakfast sausage

2 teaspoons granulated onion

2 teaspoons granulated garlic

3 tablespoons chili powder

2 teaspoons hot paprika

2 teaspoons ground cumin

2 teaspoons ground coriander

2 teaspoons cayenne pepper

2 teaspoons kosher salt

2 teaspoons freshly ground black pepper

2 cups tomato sauce

1 cup tomato paste

12 ounces beer

1 cup beef stock

2 (15.5-ounce) cans pinto beans, with juice

2 (15.5-ounce) cans kidney beans, with juice

Shane Hill

1. In large stock pot heat olive oil over medium – high heat
2. Add bell pepper, jalapeno, chilies and onion. Cook until caramelized, about 5 minutes
3. Add garlic and sauté a minute longer
4. Add meats. Cook until meat is nicely browned and cooked through, about 7 to 10 minutes
5. Add in granulated onions, granulated garlic, chili powder, paprika, cumin, coriander, cayenne, salt and pepper and cook for 1 minute
6. Add in tomato sauce and paste and stir for 2 minutes
7. Stir in beer and beef stock. Add beans, lower heat and simmer for 2 hours
8. Allow chili to cool to room temp. Freeze in vacuum seal bags
9. At the tailgate, bring a large stockpot of water to a boil
10. Add bags of chili to the water as needed. Boil for 20 minutes, remove and serve

Game 8 - Alabama vs. Tennessee

Game eight brought another away-game and the opportunity to again cook at home. Tennessee is well known as being the home of Jack Daniels and I knew I would use this in the menu. While thinking of what I was going to cook, I contacted my friend Joe who is a huge Vol's fan as well as Tennessee native. Joe told me that he will always associate country ham, moon pies and RC cola with his home state. In honor of Joe, I wanted to work these items into the menu.

Alabama always plays Tennessee in late October and I knew that I wanted to cook something hearty to go with the cool fall weather. I remember having a Smokey Mountain chicken sandwich in my younger days and wanted to capture that same spirit in a hearty dish, so I came up with Smokey Mountain chicken pasta.

I wanted to do some traditional tailgate items, but add some simple twists that would not have me over the grill all afternoon. My poached and grilled wings are a great way to limit the grill time. Poaching them ensures they are cooked and nice and juicy. Throwing them on the grill at the end gives them that great grill flavor and a nice crisp outside.

Combine all of the above, and below is the menu I came away with.

Dinner Menu

- Poached and grilled chicken wings with an RC Cola, garlic and habanero glaze
- Grilled Pork Tenderloins with homemade Jack Daniels BBQ sauce
- Smokey Mountain chicken pasta with country ham
- Moon Pie banana pudding

Poached and Grilled Chicken Wings

These have been a hit each time I cooked them. They are super easy and take away trying to get them crisp without burning them on the grill.

2 onions, quartered

2 carrots, cut in 4 sections each

Shane Hill

2 sticks celery, cut in 4 sections each

1 tablespoon whole black peppercorns

2 tablespoons salt

3 drops liquid crab boil (yes, 3 drops this stuff is potent)

3 lbs fresh chicken wings

Enough water to cover wings

1. In large stock pot, bring all spices and water to a boil
2. Reduce heat to a simmer and simmer for 10 minutes to allow spices to come together
3. Put wings in water and simmer for 25 minutes
4. Drain wings and grill over high heat to get them crunchy

RC Cola Garlic and Habanero Wing Glaze

This is a variation of a Dr. Pepper glaze I have been using for a few years. RC Cola is pretty sweet and the peppers give it a nice kick. This is also one that I taste and adjust as I go.

1 cup RC Cola

Juice of 1 lime

1 cup of brown sugar

1 habanero, diced (wear gloves)

1 clove garlic, diced

1 teaspoon oil

1. In a sauce pot, heat oil over medium heat
2. Brown garlic and pepper in oil
3. Place RC Cola, lime juice and sugar in sauce pot
4. Bring to a boil, then reduce heat and simmer 15 minutes or until thick stirring along the way
5. Serve with wings

Jack Daniels BBQ Sauce

Here is a take on a classic and easy BBQ sauce. Adding the Jack gives it a nice smoky taste and the alcohol helps release some of the tomato flavors in the sauce. I sometimes use a garlic chili sauce instead of the sweet chili sauce.

1 small onion, diced

2 cloves of garlic, diced

1 tablespoon olive oil

1 cup ketchup

1/2 cup cider vinegar

1 cup Jack Daniels

1/2 cup sweet chili sauce (from the Asian section)

1 cup brown sugar

1. Heat oil to medium –high in a saucepan. Brown onion in oil, add garlic and cook 1 more minute
2. Stir remaining ingredients into sauce pan and bring to a boil (careful adding the whiskey, if you are using gas turn the heat off to avoid a fire. Once combined, turn the heat back on)
3. Reduce heat to a simmer and cook for 30 minutes, stirring from time to time

Smokey Mountain Chicken Pasta with Country Ham

This dish plays into the traditional Smokey Mountain Sandwich. It is hearty and easy to make. Careful with the country ham as it is pretty salty. You can cheat and use rotisserie chicken meat and skip grilling the breasts.

2 chicken breast, grilled and diced

4 slices of country ham, diced

1 cup of BBQ sauce, heated

1/2 cup jack cheese, shredded

Shane Hill

4 green onions, diced

1 lb of your favorite pasta (I use linguini), cooked and drained

1. Combine all ingredients in a large bowl and toss

Moon Pie Banana Pudding

I have always liked banana pudding and Moon Pies, so why not combine both and come up with the ultimate southern dish. It taste just like it looks, delicious!

2 chocolate Moon Pies, crumbled

1 banana Moon Pie, crumbled

3 bananas, sliced

1 (3 ounce) box instant vanilla pudding

1 1/2 cups milk

1/2 can Eagle Brand Milk

4 ounces Cool Whip

1. Line 9x13 pan with crumbled Moon Pies
2. Cover with banana slices
3. Mix pudding, milk, Eagle Brand Milk and cool whip. Pour over bananas
4. Refrigerate to set

Game 9 - Alabama vs. LSU

Game nine ushered in with Alabama playing the LSU Tigers in Baton Rouge. Each year I come up with a new menu and dish for each of our games. I do not like repeating the same thing year after year. However, LSU is the one exception.

I always cook jambalaya and gumbo for this game. This is a menu that I start on the week prior and not one for the faint of heart. 9 times out of 10 when I cook something and people say 'was it a lot of work' my usual answer is 'no' and that is true. I love cooking and I love the process of planning, breaking down the food and creating something for everyone to enjoy.

Let me tell you right now, gumbo done right is one heck of a lot of work. I have tried some shortcuts to this dish in the past and they were noticed. From the roux to the stock and the sausage to the seafood, it takes time and is a true labor of love. The jambalaya requires the same attention to get the best results, but is not one that I would call involved.

Through the years I have kept some things the same and I have added others to these recipes. I have been using the same andouille for years, but grew tired of not being happy with the Tasso around here so now I make my own. I introduced duck stock to the gumbo a few years back. These are just some of the ways the recipes have evolved.

I will also caution that for the gumbo, this is only a guide and that I adjust, flavor and tweak the recipe so much each time there is no way to document it. So much of it depends on how the stocks come out. My gumbo does not contain fish because my wife is allergic to fish (it does contain shellfish).

LSU Menu

- Gumbo Ya-Ya
- Chicken and Sausage Jambalaya

Gumbo Ya-Ya (shellfish, fowl and sausage)

This is based off Emeril's Delmonico Gumbo. I adjust as I go and will vary from the recipe quite a bit at times, especially from the spices. A key to this is the roux and stock. As I

Shane Hill

make my stocks I start to season them until they taste like a good gumbo base. Also, I keep several bags of the Louisiana Brand Cajun Gumbo Mix on hand to help adjust the final taste.

3 cups very dark roux

4 whole blue crabs, cleaned and ready to cook

3 pounds good andouille sausage, cut into 1/2 inch rounds

4 lbs medium shrimp, peeled

2 dozen oysters, shucked

2 containers of crab claw meat

4 cups onions, diced

3 cups red peppers, diced

2 cups celery, diced

5 cloves garlic, diced

1 small can tomato paste

3 tablespoons fresh basil, diced

3 tablespoons fresh thyme, diced

4 bay leaves

2 beers

5 cups duck stock

5 cups shrimp stock

2 teaspoons liquid crab boil

Salt and pepper to taste

Cajun seasoning to taste

4 bags Louisiana Cajun Gumbo Mix

1. In large thick bottom stock pot, brown sausage and remove from pan
2. Bring 1/2 roux to medium heat in sausage drippings
3. Add onions, peppers and celery and cook until browned (about 10 minutes) – season with Cajun seasoning and salt and pepper
4. Stir in tomato paste, herbs and bay leaves and cook for 1 minute
5. Slowly start adding stocks stirring to incorporate, add shrimp boil and crabs
6. Bring to a boil then reduce heat to a simmer and start tasting and adjusting spices
7. Slowly add remaining roux, stirring to incorporate
8. Add sausage and crab claw meat
9. Reduce heat to a simmer and simmer for 1 hour. Taste and season along the way
10. Once the gumbo is about ready, add the shrimp and oysters and cook until shrimp are pink and the oysters start to curl

Chicken and Sausage Jambalaya

This recipe is straight up from a Bobby Flay Throwdown episode. Full credit goes to Emile Stieffel, though I do make my own Tasso for this one. I have always tripled this recipe and used my own ratio of 2 1/2 parts stock to rice.

The heavy bottom dutch oven is a key to this dish. The fresh herbs are also a must to get the best flavor.

2 lbs good andouille sausage, cut into 1/4 inch rounds

2 1/2 lbs boneless skinless chicken thigh meat

1 1/2 lbs onions, diced

2 tablespoons garlic, minced

1 lb Tasso, cubed

3/4 tablespoon whole fresh thyme leaves

3/4 tablespoon chopped fresh sweet basil leaves

1/2 tablespoon coarsely ground black pepper

1/2 tablespoon white pepper

Shane Hill

1/2 tablespoon red pepper flakes

1/3 gallon chicken stock

1 1/4 pounds long-grain rice

1 tablespoon freshly chopped curly parsley leaves

Cajun spice to taste

Large cast iron dutch oven

1. Brown sausage over medium-high heat. You may need to add a little oil
2. Add the chicken thighs and season them, continue to brown with the sausage. It should take about 20 minutes. Keep them moving with a steel spoon
3. Lower heat and add onions and garlic. Cook for about 15 minutes until clear. Scrape the bottom of the pot with the steel spoon
4. Add Tasso and spices and reduce heat to low and cook for 10 minutes to allow oils from the spices to release
5. Add stock and bring to a boil, add rice and stir to break up rice. After about 5 minutes, add parsley and stir, place lid on tight and reduce to low and cook for 25 minutes. DO NOT PEEK.

Game 10 - Alabama vs. Mississippi State

I do not miss many games. But, Julie and I had a vacation opportunity that we could not turn down during the Mississippi State game. That would put me missing two games in one year; I had only missed one game in the last eight years. We thought long and hard about it and decided we had to take the vacation.

Mr. Jarmon decided to fill in for me on this one and did a fine job. He decided to cook Brunswick Stew, so I thought what better recipe to put right here in the book. This is a combination of several recipes and includes some of my own touches.

Brunswick stew has long been one of my favorites. I was actually introduced to it when I used to spend lots of time across the state in Auburn. It is a great fall dish, rich and hearty and also has some magical powers to help cure a hangover.

This version is a cheater version since I will use store bought meat and some canned items. However, it is quick and can feed a ton of folks.

Late Fall Lunch

- Brunswick Stew

Brunswick Stew

If you have not picked up on the fact, I like to use rotisserie chicken meat for most of my chicken dishes. This one is no exception. This is a base recipe and you can take it about anyway you like.

1 rotisserie chicken, meat removed

2 lbs BBQ pork, get it from your favorite joint

3 cups chicken stock

(2) 28 ounce cans of crushed tomatoes

(2) 16 ounce cans creamed corn

1/2 cup sugar

Shane Hill

2 cups catsup

1 1/2 cups BBQ sauce

1 tablespoon liquid smoke

3 tablespoons worcestershire sauce

4 tablespoons BBQ rub

Salt and pepper to taste

1. Mix and stir all liquids and bring to a boil
2. Reduce heat to simmer and stir in meat and sugar
3. Cook for 1 hour stirring from time to time. Add more broth if it gets too thick

Game 11 - Alabama vs. Georgia State

Apparently 2010 was the year of the night game for Alabama home games. Georgia State combined the night game and our first Thursday game in some time. Since this was not going to be a huge tailgate, I decided not to take off work that day. I needed something that I could quickly whip up and feed everyone in under an hour.

In keeping with my theme of using an Alabama local product, I decided to work peaches into the mix in honor of Chilton County. I have always thought that pork and peaches go well together. Pork tenderloins are also a great way to cook for a group and get things off the grill fast. I decided to do pork with peach and mango salsa as well as a mango and pepper salsa for those that like a little more spice. In keeping with fast prep time I decided to pair it with grilled pineapple black beans and coconut rice.

For the salsas, I bought them from the store. Since I was under a pretty big time crunch, I decided to go this route and it worked out just fine.

Quick Tailgate Dinner Menu

- Grilled Pork Tenderloins Served With
  - Peach and mango salsa
  - Mango and pepper salsa
- Black Beans With Grilled Pineapple
- Coconut Rice

Grilled Pork Tenderloins

You can mix up the spices if you want a different flavor. I like to cook pork tenderloins until they have just a little pink in the middle.

2 pork tenderloins

2 tablespoons olive oil

Salt and pepper to taste

1. Toss tenderloins with oil and season with salt and pepper

2. Heat grill with a hot fire on one side and low fire on the other. Sear on all 4 sides over hot heat. Move to low heat and grill for 15-20 minutes. Internal temp should be 145 degrees when you pull it from the fire
3. Allow to rest for 5 minutes and slice into 1/2" pieces and cover with salsa

Black Beans with Grilled Pineapple

This is a quick and simple dish. Grilling the pineapple gives it a great flavor.

(2) 14 ounce cans of black beans

1 fresh pineapple prepared and ready to eat, sliced into 1/2" rounds

1 onion, diced (I bought this already prepared in the vegetable section)

1 teaspoon prepared garlic

2 tablespoons olive oil

Salt and pepper to taste

1. Heat olive oil over medium high heat in a large sauce pot
2. Cook onions for 8 minutes, add garlic and cook for 1 more minute. Season with salt and pepper as you cook them
3. Add black beans and bring to a boil, reduce heat and simmer for 10 minutes
4. While beans are simmering, grill pineapple over hot grill, about 2 minutes per side.
5. Dice grilled pineapple and stir into beans
6. Simmer for 5 minutes

Coconut Rice

This is a fast and easy dish that gives rice a little flavor. I have also mixed black beans into this dish before

2 cups rice

1 cup canned coconut milk

3 cups chicken stock

1. Add liquid and rice to a sauce pot and bring to a boil, stirring along the way
2. Reduce heat to low and cover with a tight lid and cook for 20 minutes. Do not peek along the way

Game 12 - Alabama vs. Auburn

The Auburn game is always one of my favorite tailgates because we always have a number of AU fans there. I love nothing more than to host fans from the other team and make sure they are well fed and have a great time. Our friend Chuck (aka 'Coach') is always at the AU game and if you have been there you know who he is. Chuck makes sure everyone has a great time and that everyone stays in line.

As it turned out, this was our largest tailgate of the year with over 100 folks ready to drink and eat. I wanted to make sure that we had food coming off early and that there was a variety of dishes right up until kickoff.

The core tailgate group really is family, so with the game being on the heels of Thanksgiving I thought we should have some type of family feast. I decided to have a traditional Asado as well as plenty of breakfast food and drinks. In keeping with the tradition of featuring a local Alabama ingredient I decided to grill up all the offerings from Conecuh sausage as part of the Asado. Conecuh offers a verity of sausages and is one of my staples for grilling. At home I often throw on a batch while the grill is heating to give everyone something to munch on while they are fixing the first drink of the evening.

Of course a tailgate would not be the same without a drink. This one was made up at the game by my favorite bartender and Auburn fan Clabe. With that we bring you the 'Screwy Mango Mimosa'.

Breakfast

- Screwy Mango Mimosa
- Breakfast Burritos with grilled sausages

Lunch

- Asado
  - Whole Butterflied Jamaican jerk chickens
  - Conecuh sausages
  - Grilled Flank Steak with chimichurri sauce
  - Leg of lamb
  - Roasted winter root veggies

Screwy Mango Mimosa

A huge thanks to Clabe for coming up with this one. We were originally going to make it as a standard mimosa with mango / orange, but Clabe saw the vodka and gave it a try. This will now be a staple item for our games.

4 ounces champagne, chilled

4 ounces mango / orange juice mix, chilled

1 shot chilled vodka

1. Combine, shake over ice, strain and serve

Breakfast Burritos

These are always a hit. Since I was starting the grill to get the meats cooking, why not grill some of the sausage?

This is for one burrito. I usually make up pans of each of the ingredients and let people make their own.

1 egg, scrambled

Grilled sausage (I use a mix of breakfast links and smoked Cajun sausage)

1/4 onion, sautéed

1/4 red pepper, sautéed

2 tablespoons salsa

2 tablespoons Mexican cheese

1 large tortilla

1. Stuff tortilla with ingredients and enjoy

Jamaican Jerked Butterflied Chicken

Removing the backbone is easy with a good pair of kitchen shears and allows for a quicker cooking bird. Try this with any of your favorite chicken rubs or marinades.

Shane Hill

1 whole chicken, backbone removed and pressed flat to where the breast bone breaks

4 tablespoons olive oil

4 tablespoons dry jerked seasoning

1. Rub chicken in oil
2. Rub spices on and under the skin
3. Place chicken in zip lock bag and refrigerate overnight
4. Prepare grill with one side hot and the other side for indirect cooking
5. Sear chicken on both sides over hot fire, move to indirect side of grill and cook until done. The USDA recommends 165 degrees at the thickest part of the breast and thigh.

Grilled Conecuh Sausages

These are always a hit and they have the extra bonus of being an Alabama product. Try tossing them with BBQ sauce after they come off the grill.

Several varied packages of Conecuh sausages

1. Heat grill to medium
2. Add sausage and brown on all sides, careful about flare ups

Grilled Flank Steak

Flank steak has a reputation of being tough. Cook it high and fast with a little citrus and then slice it against the grain and it is wonderful.

1 flank steak

1 tablespoon olive oil

Salt and fresh ground pepper to coat

1 lime, juiced

1. Rub steak with lime juice
2. Rub steak with oil
3. Sprinkle both sides with salt and pepper
4. Heat grill to high

5. Sear steak on both sides for 3 minutes
6. Move to cooker section of grill and cook for another 4 – 8 minutes. I think it is best medium rare
7. Slice against the grain with an angle cut so that each bite has a large section of outer bark

Roasted Leg of Lamb

I first tried this dish a few years ago for our Christmas party and it was a hit. I sometimes use fajita or mojo seasoning for this one as well. People who love lamb line up for this one and I have converted several people who claimed to hate lamb.

1 deboned leg of lamb

5 tablespoons olive oil

4 tablespoons minced rosemary

4 tablespoons minced garlic

Salt and pepper to taste

1. Combine oil, garlic and rosemary to make a paste
2. Rub leg of lamb with paste and salt and pepper
3. Setup grill for indirect cooking with one side high and the other side very low
4. Sear leg of lamb over high heat and move to indirect / low side
5. Cover and grill until done. I like mine medium rare (145 degrees)

Roasted Winter Root Veggies

This is an easy side dish that pairs well with the various grilled meats.

2 pounds of sweet potatoes, peeled and diced into 1" cubes

1 pound fresh Brussels sprouts, cut into halves

1 pack of carrots, peeled and cut into 1" sections

1 pack of parsnips, peeled and cut into 1" sections

4 pears, cored and cut into quarters

Shane Hill

2 tablespoons olive oil

Salt and pepper to taste

1. Heat oven or grill to 350 degrees
2. Place all vegetables but pears into a disposable roasting pan
3. Toss with oil and salt and pepper
4. Roast in oven for 30 minutes
5. Add pears to mixture and roast for 30 minutes more

Game 13 - Alabama vs. Michigan State

Just like that the 2010 season came and went. What a crazy year it turned out to be. Back to back Heisman trophy winners and nation champions from the same state. For the last tailgate of the season I wanted to once again work some things from the opposing team into the menu. With the game falling on New Year's Day I wanted to serve greens, black eyed peas and hog jaw in some form.

When I started researching Michigan, I found that there were several things I could work into the menu. They are known for their apples, cherries and mint, and they indeed brought us Vernor's ginger ale. So why not work all these into the menu? I also wanted to keep something from Alabama in the menu and in this case decided to use Alabama Wild Gulf Shrimp. If you are here in Birmingham, give Snapper Grabbers a call for your shrimp and seafood needs. Pat and the gang are great to deal with and have wonderful fresh seafood.

For the cherries, I decided on using them in Bama Bombs paired with a Crimson Sunrise Mimosa to wash them down with. For the shrimp, I made kabobs using the shrimp and apples and finished them with a Ginger Ale glaze. In keeping with both the mint and New Years theme, I added citrus mint marinated grilled pork tenderloin and paired them with Hoppin John's and spicy greens with sausage.

New Year's Game day Menu

- Bama Bombs
- Crimson Sunrise Mimosas
- Alabama Shrimp Kabobs with Ginger Ale Glaze
- Grilled Pork Tenderloin with Citrus Mint Marinade
- Shane's Hoppin John
- Spicy Greens with Hog Jaw and Sausage

Bama Bombs

These are trouble and I mean t-r-o-u-b-l-e. They need to sit at least 2 days and will keep for a couple of months.

1 jar cherries

Shane Hill

1 bottle of pure grain alcohol

1. Pour out the juice from the cherries
2. Fill the jar with PGA
3. Let refrigerate at least 48 hours
4. Serve to your brave friends
5. Do not go near open flame for at least 10 minutes after eating

Crimson Sunrise Mimosa's

This was my twist on the tequila sunrise and was a nice way to kick off New Years Day. If you want it sweeter give grenadine a try. I found they were perfect just as listed below.

750 ml chilled champagne

350 ml chilled cranberry juice

350 ml chilled orange juice

1. Combine and serve

Alabama Shrimp and Apple Kabobs with Ginger Ale Glaze

This dish combined both Alabama and Michigan ingredients. The flavor of the ginger ale glaze gives them a nice mild spice.

1 lb shrimp Alabama Wild Shrimp, peeled and deveined

3 apples cored and cut into 1" cubes

2 tablespoons olive oil

Salt and pepper to taste

Ginger Ale Glaze (recipe follows)

1. Alternate shrimp and apples on grill safe skewers
2. Brush shrimp and apples with olive oil and sprinkle with salt and pepper
3. Place skewer on medium – high grill and grill for 3 min, flip and grill 3 min more
4. Brush with glaze and grill for 1 minute, flip and brush with glaze again and remove after 1 minute

Ginger Ale Glaze

1 cup ginger ale

1 tablespoons Dijon mustard

1 tablespoon honey

1 tablespoon butter

Dash of hot sauce

1. Combine ingredients in sauce pan and bring to a boil
2. Cook until reduced into a light glaze

Citrus Mint Marinated Grilled Pork Tenderloin

This is a super easy dish and offers a twist on traditional pork.

1 pork tenderloin

1 cup orange juice

1 lemon, juiced

1 lime, juiced

1/2 cup mint leaves, diced

2 tablespoons balsamic vinegar

Olive oil to coat

Salt and pepper to taste

1. Combine juices, mint and vinegar in a Ziploc bag. Add pork and refrigerate for three hours
2. Remove pork and pat dry. Toss in olive oil and sprinkle with salt and pepper
3. Heat grill with a hot fire on one side and low fire on the other. Sear on all 4 sides over hot heat. Move to low heat and grill for 15-20 minutes. Internal temp should be 145 degrees when you pull it from the fire.

51

Shane Hill

Shane's Hoppin John

This is my take on a traditional dish. I like to add smoked sausage to the dish for a little extra spice. This is another dish that I taste and adjust as I go.

1 pound quality smoked sausage, cut into 1/2" pieces

1 onion, diced

1/2 cup red peppers, diced

1 clove garlic, minced

1 pound black eyed peas, soaked and ready to cook

Chicken stock to cover

Bay Leaf

Salt and pepper to taste

Couple of dashes of hot sauce

1. In a large stock pot, brown sausage for 3 minutes over medium – high heat
2. Remove sausage from pan and add onion, celery and peppers and cook until transparent. Add garlic and cook for one more minute
3. Add remaining ingredients and bring to a boil
4. Reduce heat to a simmer and cook for 50 minutes or until peas are done. Season along the way with salt, pepper and hot sauce
5. Serve with cooked rice

Spicy Greens with Hog Jaw and Sausage

These greens have converted many folks who claim not to like greens. My key is a little liquid shrimp boil – be careful, this stuff is potent and I am pretty sure you can power the space shuttle off one gallon of this stuff.

1 pound quality smoked sausage, cut into 1/2" pieces

1/4 pound of hog jaw bacon (regular bacon is also fine)

2 onions, julienned

5 cloves garlic, minced

(1) 12 ounce beer

1 quart of chicken stock, may need more

4 drops shrimp boil

1/4 cup rice wine vinegar

2 tablespoons molasses

5 pounds of mixed greens

1. In a large stock pot, brown sausage for 3 minutes over medium – high heat
2. Add bacon, reduce heat to medium and continue to brown. Cook till bacon is crisp
3. Remove bacon and sausage from pan and add onion, celery and peppers and cook till transparent. Add garlic and cook for one more minute
4. Add all liquid and spices and bring to a boil
5. Slowly start adding greens to the mixture. They will wilt and you can get all 5 pounds in after some time
6. Reduce heat to a simmer and simmer for 1 1/2 hours. Taste and adjust as they go. If the liquid starts to cook out, add more stock or water

Shane Hill

Index

8365864R0

Made in the USA
Charleston, SC
02 June 2011